ALASKA
YUKON

JOSEF HANUS & JOSEF M. HANUS

Personal gift to :

From :

© *JH. Fine Art Photo Ltd.*

Mentasta Mountains

This autumn coloured valley of the Chisana River and the Mentasta Mountains is the first beautiful view of Tetlin National Wildlife Refuge, travelling to Alaska via the Alaska Highway. Several viewpoints give good opportunities for observing wildlife in the valley. Established in 1980 and covering over 730,000 acres, Tetlin NWR has a very high density of wildlife.

2

Alaska Glaciers

Alaska has 100,000 glaciers, covering over 30,000 square miles. Many glaciers are easily accessible to tourists, but most of the big glaciers can only be seen from the air. A part of Portage glacier is the subject of this photo.

Worthington Glacier

A part of Worthington Glacier can be seen close to Thompson Pass, via the Richardson Hwy.

3

Mount Drum

At 12,010 feet high, Mt.Drum is a part of the Wrangell Mountains. These photographs were taken from Chistochina.

Mt. Sanford

16,237 ft. high Mt. Sanford is located 30 miles east of Mt. Drum.

4

Valdez

Valdez Arm was first explored by the Spanish in 1790. One hundred years later, the area was utilized as a stepping stone to the Yukon gold fields, and today, the city of Valdez is nestled at its head. The ice-free Valdez Channel is an important shipping center for Alaska. The southern terminal for the 1290 km long Trans-Alaska Pipeline (lower photo) is located here, in a natural fjord of Prince William Sound.

5

Alaska

King Mountains

A spectacular view of the King Range, a part of the Chugach Mountains, rising above the Matanuska River. This view-point is near Moose Creek.

Matanuska River

Flowing through the King Range.

Alaska

Thompson Pass

The highest point of the Richardson Hwy, Thompson Pass connects Anchorage with Valdez. With an elevation of 2771 ft, it was named by Captain Abercrombie in 1899.

Blueberry Lake

Blueberry Lake is located in Thompson Pass.

7

Haines Bay

The community of Haines is located between Chilkat Inlet and Chilkoot Inlet, in the Lynn Canal. The area is surrounded by the Boundary Range and Takhinsha Mountains.

Skagway

This small port at the north end of the Inside Passage became an important gateway for thousands of gold seekers heading for Dawson City at the time of the Klondike Gold Rush in 1898.

8

Alaska

Haines Highway

The St. Elias Mountains and Haines Highway connect Skagway with Haines Junction. Three Guardsmen Pass is the highest point on the Haines Highway.

Chilkat Inlet

Mount Emerich, the Takhinsha Mountains, and Chilkat Inlet are shown in this picture.

9

Kachemak Bay

This world famous part of Cook Inlet is a favourite destination for travelers and sport anglers. Located in the south-western part of Kenai Peninsula, the beautiful beaches of Kachemak Bay are surrounded by glaciated peaks of the Kenai Mountains.

10

Homer's Harbour

Homer's Harbour on Kachemak Bay is the home port of recreational boaters and commercial fishermen. Located on the southeast point of the Sterling Highway, this beautiful port gives good recreation possibilities on beaches or browsing around numerous picturesque gift shops and sea-food restaurants. Big salmon and halibut are a common catch and a contest for the biggest fish caught is held every summer.

Kenai Peninsula

Thousands of tourists visit Kenai
Peninsula monthly in the summer, travelling along the Sterling Hwy to Homer.
Forest and tundra allow easy, close-up
views of wildlife. Hiking trails and cruises
provide opportunities for tourism and
outdoor sports.

Kenai Mountains

Kenai River

Numerous lakes and rivers on the Kenai Peninsula are famous for their fantastic fresh water sport fishing. The biggest King salmon can be caught here.

Kenai Lake

13

Kodiak Island

Situated in the Gulf of Alaska, and separated from the Alaska Peninsula by Shelikof Strait, Kodiak Island was settled by A. Baranof in 1792. It is the second largest island in the United States and home to the famous Kodiak Bear. The "Island Terrific in the North Pacific," as it is known, can be reached by Alaska State Ferry, airplane, or private boat.

Sheep Mountains

Shelikof Strait

Rich coastal waters, washing thousands of miles of untamed Alaska coastline and the shores of Kodiak Island, are a popular destination for commercial and sport anglers. The area is one of the richest fishing sites in the world.

Seward

The fishing and shipping town of Seward was established in 1903. Located in year-round ice-free Resurrection Bay, it is an important port for Alaska.

Nenana River

The Clearwater Mountains, a part of the Alaska Range, and Nenana River can be observed from Denali and Parks Highways.

Denali National Park

Originally named McKinley National Park, it was established in 1917. Mount McKinley, North America's highest peak at 20,320 ft. can be seen from the park road, the Parks Hwy. or from as far away as Anchorage.

16

Anchorage

Knik Arm in Cook Inlet is home to Alaska's largest city, founded in the 1900's as a supply centre for the Alaska Railroad. The city is surrounded by the Chugach Range and Kenai Mountains. Anchorage's population grew during the Second World War and then again when the Trans-Alaska Pipeline was constructed in 1970. The city outfitted thousands of workers who flooded into Alaska from the south. Anchorage is a beautiful, modern city and the site of Alaska Pacific University.

17

Chugach Mountains

Spreading from Cook Inlet to Jeffery Glacier, the Chugach Range reaches down to meet the waters of Prince William Sound. Bagley Icefield and Columbia Glacier are part of these mountains.

Valdez Arm

The northernmost part of Prince William Sound, Valdez Arm is home to the port of Valdez. Some forty tankers filled with oil from Prudhoe Bay in the north leave the port monthly.

18

Prince William Sound

Captain James Cook named this part of the Pacific Ocean after Prince William in 1778. Two thousand square miles of P.W.S. borders pristine wilderness and 4,000 miles of tidewater glaciers. In 1989 more than 1,300 miles of shoreline were damaged by the worst oil spill in U.S. history.

College Fjord

A point of interest in P.W.S. is the College Fjord. Every glacier in the fjord is named after an American university.

19

Alaska

Columbia Glacier

One of Alaska's most popular glaciers, Columbia is a part of the Chugach Mountains and is over 10 miles long and 25 miles wide. Rising high above Prince William Sound, Columbia Glacier can be seen beautifully from the air or partially from the sea.

Portage Glacier

Part of the Kenai Mountains, Portage Glacier is one of the most visible and most popular Alaskan glaciers. It is located close to Anchorage. Under the glacier, Portage Glacier Lake is connected by Turnagain Arm to Cook Inlet. Portage can be reached from Anchorage or Seward via Seward Highway.

Fairbanks

Alaska's second largest city, Fairbanks is known as the Golden Heart City. Nestled in the centre of the state and located at the crossroads of five highways—Richardson, Elliott, Steese, Parks and Dalton—Fairbanks is truly the heart of Alaska. The monument of Alaska's Unknown First Family stands on the bank of the Chena River.

Gold Rush

Gold miner Andy Wescott, owner of the Gold Rush Gold Camp in Fox holds a gold nugget worth $20,000!

22

Koykuk River

Dalton Hwy. begins in Livengood near Fairbanks. The highway leads the traveller through unspoiled, natural beauty. Koykuk River and the Ray Mountains were photographed near Old Man Camp.

Endicott Mountains

Endicott Mountains are a part of the Brooks Range, continental divide and border Alaska's north slope.

23

Dalton Highway

The longest route in Alaska, connecting Prudhoe Bay and Deadhorse with Fairbanks is gravel. The surface is vastly changing, in parts terribly rough, and the expression of 'Haul Road' is quite realistic.

Trans-Alaska Pipeline

It cost $8 billion to build the 1290 km long pipeline from Prudhoe Bay to Valdez. Constructed in the 1970s by 70,000 workers, the pipeline is now owned by 7 companies with 1000 employees. The oil from Prudhoe Bay fills 40 tankers monthly in Valdez.

24

Atigun Pass

At 4800ft, Atigun Pass in the Brooks Range is the highest point on the Dalton Hwy. The continental divide passes through Atigun Pass, which is the highest highway pass in Alaska.

Brooks Range

From the Chikuchi Sea to Beauford Sea spans the Brooks Range, including Schwatka, Endicott, Philip Smith, Romanzof, Davidson, British, Waring and De Long Mountains.

Alaska Cotton

Cottongrass, the main source of food for Porcupine Caribou, is common along the roads and lakes of the north. It is a member of the sedge family.

Arctic Circle

Located on the Dalton Hwy, the Arctic Circle Gateway is a popular tourist stop. At this latitude, the sun doesn't set on the summer solstice on June 21, and doesn't rise on the winter solstice on December 21.

26

Philip Smith Mountains

Travelling along Dalton Highway towards Prudhoe Bay, the Philip Smith Mountains are on the right just before rising into Atigun Pass. As a part of the Brooks Range, the mountains are the gateway to the Arctic. Here, the continental divide separates the watersheds that flow northward into the Arctic Ocean, from those that flow south and west into the Bering Sea.

27

Alaska

Romanzof Mountains

Driving beyond Atigun Pass, the Romanzof Mountains appear on the east side of the highway. After twenty kilometres, the land slowly transforms into flat tundra.

28

Deadhorse/Prudhoe Bay

The purely industrial town of Deadhorse was established to support oil development in Prudhoe Bay, where super-rich oil fields with an estimated reserve of 10 billions barrels of crude oil were discovered in 1968.

Midnight Sun

"Sunset" and "sunrise" above Prudhoe Bay were photographed using multiple exposures, between 2 AM and 4 AM. Here on the 70th parallel, the sun doesn't set for 82 days in summer and doesn't rise for 66 days in winter.

29

Alaska

Baranof Island

The first peoples here were Tlingit Indians. Russian settlers came to the Sitka site for its economic potential, with timbered forests and fur trading. The natives attacked Baranof's people in 1802, but were later driven off. Russia sold Alaska to the United States for $7.2 million in gold, here in Sitka on October 18, 1867. Sitka then became the capital of Alaska until 1900.

Sitka

St Michael's Russian Orthodox Cathedral.

30

Ketchikan

Established in 1887, the fourth largest community in Alaska is known as the salmon capital of the world. The first salmon cannery was built in 1887. Ketchikan is nestled on Revillagigedo Island in Clarence Strait, and is an important fishing and logging city.

Creek Street

Alaska's most notorious red-light district (from 1902 to 1954) is a destination of historical interest for tourists.

31

Mendenhall Glacier

Mendenhall Glacier is a part of the Coastal Mountains. It can be reached by hiking several kilometers from Juneau.

Juneau

Joe Juneau and Richard Harris found gold on October 1880 and laid claim to the area which they called Gold Creek. It was the largest find of the Alaska Gold Rush era. Juneau, the Capital city of Alaska since 1900, is beautifully set between Mt. Juneau and Mt. Roberts.

32

Saxman Village

A settlement of the Alaska native Tlingit peoples, Saxman Village is located 5 km south of Ketchikan. The village and its collection of totems and the exhibit of a Tlingit totem carver's workshop is a favorite tourist attraction.

Hubbard Glacier

Alaska's most beautiful and largest tide-water glacier flows into Yakutat Bay as a part of Malaspina Glacier.

33

Klondike Plateau

Boundary Mountains on the Alaska-Yukon border.

Chicken

Quaint downtown Chicken can be reached travelling along the Tailor Hwy. to Canada's boundary.

Butte Creek Dredge

First bucketline dredge, installed in 1934 on Butte Creek.

Tintina Trench

The mountains enclosing the Klondike Valley above Dawson City are the nicest and most colourful in the fall, shown here in early September.

Klondike Plateau

The eastern end of the plateau descends into Dawson City.

Dawson Range

Numerous abandoned communities and many in complete solitude are scattered throughout the Dawson Range and the Klondike Plateau, around the Yukon River valley.

Next to Jack London's cabin under Reindeer Mountain, there are small communities such as Thistle Creek, Coffee Creek, Issac Creek, Sewart River and Fort Selkirk, all prospector settlements on the Yukon River.

36

Top of the World

The name of this route was inspired by the topographic position of the road on the ridge of the Klondike Plateau. 70 km westward from Dawson City to the border with Alaska, the Top of the World Highway winds along the ridgetop of the Klondike Plateau. In the fall, the mountainsides change to amazing red and yellow colours. Simply a fantastic experience.

Yukon

Jack London's Cabin

Jack London, the famous Gold Rush-era writer of the North is very closely connected to Dawson City. His cabin is still here on 8th Ave, close to Klondike and Yukon Rivers.

Dawson City

Arriving for the first time via the Klondike Highway to a nighttime Dawson City, and seeing the Northern Lights on the black sky is an unforgettable experience. Dawson City is a unique, beautiful and romantic place in Canada's North.

38

Dawson City

The heart of the Klondike Gold Rush is a place of living history. In 1900, 30,000 gold seekers transformed an Indian fishing camp into a large city. Original and renovated houses from the Gold Rush era remind tourists of its glamorous, world-famous history.

Robert Service

The cabin of Gold Rush poet Robert Service is located on 8th Ave, close to Dawson's cemetery.

39

Grand Forks

The place where 10,000 prospectors lived in log houses around Bonanza and Eldorado Creeks and worked on their claims or for larger mining companies, is now empty. Just huge piles of stones, where dredges worked and ruins of homes remind tourists that here lived many thousands of people who all caught the same rush—the gold rush…

A Prospector's Home

Ruins remaining around Grand Forks remind us of the first settlers, the Klondike Gold Rush prospectors.

40

Dawson's Cemetaries

Several cemetaries, one on 8th Ave in the city and the others high above the Klondike Valley, are the final resting places for thousand of gold seekers, who arrived from the south to Dawson City with just one thought—finding gold and becoming rich. Some of them did it, but thousands found only hard work and disappointment, such as Dave Sicklesteel. Born in Detroit in 1865, he came to Dawson City in 1901 and lost his life four years later, in March 1905.

41

Klondike Valley Rivers

The heart of the Klondike valley is the confluence of the Yukon and Klondike Rivers, photographed here from the Top of the World Hwy. This photograph shows the whole Klondike Valley with the confluence of both rivers, Bear Creek, Rock Creek and King Solomon Dome Mountain.

Tintina Trench

Hills above Dawson city and Yukon River Valley.

Yukon

Bonanza Creek

An incredible 45 pounds of gold per day could be produced by *Gold Dredge #4* on *Claim 67 Below*. The largest mining companies built huge dredges to dig larger quantities of gold from the riverbed, as deep as 48 feet below the water. Some two dozen big dredges operated in the area, in locales such as Hunker and Bonanza Creeks, and on the Klondike River itself.

Gold Panning

Try your luck—free gold panning for visitors is allowed on Bonanza Creek.

43

Dempster Highway

The 740 km long Dempster Hwy. winds around Ogilvie and Thombstone Mountains, along Richardson and Wernecke Mountains. Passing rivers, lakes and unending plains, the highway crosses the Arctic Circle and one time-zone. The Dempster connects the Yukon with Canada's most northern large city of Inuvik. The experience of a trip in this part of the Yukon is breathtaking. The Dempster Highway is open year-round.

44

Yukon

Wernecke Mountains

The expansive range of the Wernecke Mountains is spread out across the centre of the Yukon. The Northern end touches the Arctic Circle and the East borders with the Mackenzie Mountains in the Northwest Territories.

Blackstone River Valley

Coloured by the fall, Blackstone River Valley can be observed from several viewpoints along the Dempster Hwy.

Thombstone Mountains

The Thombstone Mountains are a part of the Ogilvie Mountains. They are the first ridge passed when driving north along Dempster Highway.

Nordfork Pass Summit

The highest point on the Dempster Hwy. is 4265 feet. In the centre of the Thombstone Mountain skyline is a needle-like peak with an elevation of 7200 feet.

46

Ogilvie Mountains

Autumn paints the Yukon's plains and hills with beautiful colours of red and orange. This photograph of Mt. Klotz *(left)* were taken near Engineer Creek.

Nahanni Range

Melting snow fills wide lakes on upland plains with good drinking water for wildlife.

Yukon

Sapper Hill

Sapper Hill, with its eroding pillars rises above Engineer Creek and Ogilvie River. The place is located in the Ogilvie Mountains.

Ogilvie River

Flowing along the Dempster Highway, Ogilvie River offers good Arctic Graylink and Trout fishing.

48

Engineer Creek

Sulfur springs, with their typical smell and the red colouring on the banks of Engineer Creek from iron oxide are an interesting geological feature of the mountains along Dempster Highway.

Peel River Valley

Peel River and Wernecke Mountains.

49

Richardson Mountains

Spreading from the Mackenzie Delta to Peel River Valley, Richardson Mountains are the gateway to the Northwest Territories when travelling via Dempster Highway to Inuvik. A beautiful panorama can be seen from the Arctic Circle Gateway.

Arctic Circle Gateway

Thirty kilometers north of Eagle Plains this favourite tourist destination is reached, where the sun doesn't set on June 21 and doesn't rise on December 21.

50

Eagle River

Located in the valley between Eagle Plains and the Arctic Circle Gateway.

Eagle Plains

The midpoint of the Dempster Hwy, Eagle Plains is an oasis on Yukon's longest route, offering hotel lodging, fuel and any necessary car service. This picture of the tundra was taken near the village of Eagle Plains.

Yukon

Tagish Lake

Klondike Highway connects Skagway with Whitehorse and Dawson City. Passing through the Coastal Mountains, the highway winds along Tagish Lake. Bowe Island is on the left side of this picture. The waters of Tagish and Marsh Lakes are the source the Yukon River.

Carcross

The pioneer town Carcross, formerly known as Caribou Crossing, was a stopping point for gold stampeders travelling to the Klondike Valley.

52

Atlin Lake

This crystal clear lake, located partially in B.C.'s Coast Mountains, was the location of the richest gold strike made during the great rush era. Miners' camps around the lake, such as Scotia Bay and Taku, were abandoned after the deposits of gold became less profitable. The town of Atlin, founded in 1898, is now a favourite centre for water sport lovers.

Emerald Lake

A magically colored lake near the community of Robinson, shines like a green jewel by the Klondike Hwy.

53

Yukon

Alaska Highway

The Highway, at 2500 km in length, stretches from Dawson Creek, B.C., to Fairbanks, Alaska. As a part of the U.S. defense system, The Alaska Hwy. was constructed in 8 months in 1942, by 10,000 American troopers.

Swift River

Located by the Alaska Highway, in the southern part of the Yukon, on the border with British Columbia.

54

Rancheria Falls

Rancheria River Valley and Rancheria Falls are a favorite tourist stop on the Alaska Highway.

Watson Lake

Signpost Forest, Watson Lake's best known attraction, was started in 1942 by homesick U.S. army troopers, pointing the way home.

Miles Canyon

Miles Canyon is cut by the Yukon River, with a popular landscape point of interest near Schwatka Lake, close to Whitehorse, just 1 km off the Alaska Highway.

Yukon River

The Yukon River, photographed near Five Finger Rapids.

56

Whitehorse

The home to 25,000 people, Whitehorse was incorporated as a city in 1950 and became the capital of the Yukon in 1953. Set in a mountain valley, this community was founded in 1898, as a stopping place for gold prospectors streaming through during the Gold Rush.

S.S. Klondike

The last sternwheeler, the S.S. Klondike operated on the Yukon River. Now it is anchored in Whitehorse as a river transport museum.

Yukon

Kluane National Park

Canada's highest mountains, the St. Elias Range and their highest peak, 5959m Mt. Logan, can be seen from the Alaska Hwy, near 60 km long Kluane Lake. The Kluane Museum of Natural History in the small village of Burwash Landing and Kluane Wilderness Village are much sought destinations for tourism and recreation in this area.Visitors who come for flightseeing tours can see the St. Elias Mountains and the Kluane, Stelle, Lowell and Kaskawuish Glaciers from the air.

Yukon

Champagne

Located on Dalton trail, 90 km west of Whitehorse, Champagne was a North West Mounted Police detachment. The small town is now almost deserted. This fall picture was taken between Champagne and Canyon Creek.

Fish Lake

Near Whitehorse, and located under Mt. Arkell, is this small lake.

59

Five Finger Rapids

The Yukon River flows through a spot near Carmack where the river is split by four sandstone columns into five separate streams.

Ogilvie Mountains

Klondike River Valley and the Ogilvie Mountains in the background were photographed from the viewpoint near Dempster Gateway.

Yukon River

A ringing word in the 1900's, the Yukon River flows from Marsh Lake to Whitehorse, then passes through the Klondike Plateau to Dawson City, adding to the waters of the Klondike River and then continues with a strong current to Alaska where it empties into the Bering Sea at the end of its 1500 km journey.

Montague Roadhouse

A typical roadhouse, where lodging and food was provided during the Gold Rush. Located between Whitehorse and Dawson City.

61

Yukon

Elsa

A Swedish miner staked his claim where silver was discovered in 1901 and named this site Elsa. The community grew up in 1919 and the local mine operation was the richest silver mine in North America. In 1988, the price of silver fell and mines were closed.

Silver Trail

A sunset over Mt. Hadlane, from the Silver Trail Highway, close to the abandoned mining town of Elsa.

Keno Hill

Ruins of a miner's home and a small stone monument remain at the top of Keno Hill high above McQuesten Valley, a legacy of rich silver mines of the 1920's. Several hiking trails lead to the summit of 1850m.

Keno City

Silver Trail Highway ends in Keno, a romantic town with population of 26 people. Keno Mining Museum is the main tourist attraction.

63

South Canol Road

The most interesting road in the Yukon, this 220km one lane gravel road is closed in the winter and on rainy days and is not recommended for RVs. It was constructed in 1942 to provide access to oil fields in N.W.T. The oil project was abandoned in 1945 and Canol Road was declared a National Historic Site. After passing Macmillan Pass, the road continues as North Canol Road into N.W.T., and is strictly closed to motor vehicles.

Anvil Range

A photo of wildflowers from Canol Rd.

Mayo

Riverboat traffic on the Stewart River was an important delivery system for supplying local mine operators. Mayo, settled in 1900, was a river steamer dock. Riverboat traffic ended in 1949, when the Silver Trail Highway was opened.

Pelly Crossing

Home to the Selkirk Indian Band, located on Pelly River near the Klondike Highway.

65

Big Salmon Range

Big Salmon Range is a part of the Pelly Mountains. The Yukon River surges through the high cliffs, creating many islands and interesting possibilities for canoeing.

Mayo River

The Mayo River near the town of Mayo. The town of Mayo records the greatest annual temperature variation in Canada.

66

Lake Laberge

Fascinating Yukon vegetation follows tourists at each step, in every season. Hundreds of different kinds of flowers in a spectrum of colors, lighted by the oblique red-yellow Yukon night sun is a unique experience. This photograph was taken on the Yukon Plateau, near Lake Laberge.

Miners Range

Miners Range near Fox Lake.

Wright Pass Summit

The gate to the Northwest Territories via the Dempster Highway is Wright Pass Summit, located in the Richardson Mountains some 30 km north of the Arctic Circle at an elevation of 853m.

Richardson Mountains

The Richardson Mountains are located in the most northwestern part of the Northwest Territories.

68

Arctic Red River

Scenic photo of a lake nearby.

Fort McPherson

The Lost Patrol gravesite at the local cemetery of the Anglican Church has a short, sad story. In December 1910, Inspector Fitzgerald and three men left the post with mail for Dawson City, a distance of over 500km to the South. Because of the polar night, the patrol lost their direction and all four men were found frozen 14 months later by Corporal Dempster. In his honour the road was named the Dempster Highway.

Inuvik

The Mackenzie Delta is the home of Canada's most northern city. Founded in the 1950's by the federal government as a supply centre for a military project and later for the oil boom, Inuvik is located at the Northern tip of the Dempster Hwy. It is the most visited town in the northern Arctic.

Our Lady of Victory Church

Shaped like an igloo against the climate, Inuvik's town church is built from wooden panels, painted white.

70

South Nahanni River

Nahanni National Park was the first place in the world to be designated a National Heritage Site in 1978. The 150 km long park with its spectacular Virginia Falls, great wilderness and challenging whitewater kayaking is situated around the South Nahanni River, between Thunder Cloud and Tlogotsho Ranges.

Fort Simpson

A small community, located in western part of N.W.T., by the confluence of the Liard and Mackenzie Rivers.

71

Great Slave Lake

The fifth largest lake in North America, Great Slave Lake is an important transport link for Yellowknife and Hay River and commercial trout fishing. Its beautiful beaches are much sough after in the summer. Frozen in winter, the lake shortens travel for reaching remote villages on the lake's opposite shore.

Yellowknife Bay

The closest part of the lake to the city, with its numerous small islands, Yellowknife Bay is truly the living heart of Yellowknife.

Yellowknife

The capital of the Northwest Territories is located on the north shore of Great Slave Lake. It is named after yellow bladed copper knives used by its first native residents. The town was growing in 1930 when gold was found nearby. Yellowknife became the capital in 1967. The population of this modern and young community is still growing. Some parts of the old town are still in the style of its pioneer days.

Wood Buffalo Park

Canada's largest, Wood Buffalo National Park was established in 1922 to protect the last remaining free roaming wood bison in North America. Visitors to the park can see unique salt plains, numerous species of wildlife and this geologically interesting sink hole, formed by ground water erosion.

Salt Plains

74

Fort Liard

A small village nestled in the valley of the Liard River, close to the border with Yukon and British Columbia.

Liard River Crossing

Liard River Crossing is located on the Mackenzie Highway, near Fort Simpson. The waters of Liard River empty into the Mackenzie River.

75

Louise Falls

Scenic and unique, Alexandra, Louise, and Lady Evelyn Falls are located on the Hay River, a few kilometres under the community of Enterprise, close to the border with Alberta.

Hay River

Springing from the interior plains of Alberta, Hay River crosses the border of B.C. and later empties into Great Slave Lake.

Mackenzie River

1730km long Mackenzie River is the longest river in Canada. Starting from Great Slave Lake, the river flows through the N.W.T., draining the waters of thousands of rivers and creeks and ends at the Mackenzie Delta near Inuvik where it empties into the Beauford Sea. It is the world's largest river system. This picture was taken from the ferry, crossing the river near Fort Providence.

Fort Providence Church

This trapping community was established in 1861.

Mackenzie Route

Named for explorer A. Mackenzie who sailed in 1779 to the mouth of the Mackenzie River, seeking a trade route for the Hudson's Bay Company. The route is over 2000 km long and connects almost all the communities in the N.W.T. to the Liard and Alaska Hwy and to Alberta's highway system. The route is open all year round.

Hay River

This small modern town is the major port in the N.W.T. and the centre of Great Slave Lake's fishing industry. An old Hudson Bay Company store was originally on the east side of the river.

78

Saamba Deh Falls

Dramatic Saamba Deh Falls, located in Territorial park on the Trout River are a fascinating spectacle.

Northern Lakes

Thousands of lakes and many remote communities in the northern part of the N.W.T. can only be reached by air.

79

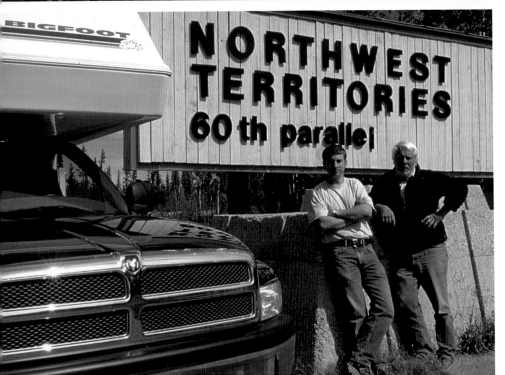

Slave River

A river veteran, resting on the bank of Slave River in Fort Smith was the last photograph taken on our memorable, many month–long photographic trip through Alaska, Yukon and the Northwest Territories.

—*Josef Hanus*

Leaving the North

The authors of this book, Josef Hanus Jr. and Josef Hanus, photographed on Alberta's northern border.